MW01106066

EXTREME SUMMER
SPORTS ZONE

MOTO X BEST TRICK

Patrick G. Cain

Lerner Publications Company • Minneapolis

Lerner Publications Company
A division of Lerner Publishing Group, Inc.
241 First Avenue North
Minneapolis, MN 55401 U.S.A.

Website address: www.lernerbooks.com

Content Consultant: Jason Weigandt, Senior Editor, *Racer X Illustrated*

Library of Congress Cataloging-in-Publication Data

Cain, Patrick G.
    Moto X best trick / by Patrick G. Cain.
       p.   cm. — (Extreme summer sports zone)
    Includes index.
    ISBN 978–1–4677–0752–7 (lib. bdg. : alk. paper)
    1. Stunt cycling—Juvenile literature. 2. Motocross—Juvenile literature. 3. ESPN
X-Games—Juvenile literature. I. Title.
    GV1060.154.C35 2013
    796.6—dc23   2012025602

Manufactured in the United States of America
1 – BP – 12/31/12

Photo credits: The images in this book are used with the permission of: Backgrounds: © Pospisil MRL/Shutterstock Images, 4-5, 15; © Harry How/Getty Images, 6; © Jeff Crow/iStockphoto, 7; © AP Images, 9; © Phil Sandlin/AP Images, 10; © Stew Milne/AP Images, 11; © J. S. Moses/AP Images, 12; © Lenny Ignelzi/Shutterstock Images, 13, 18; © Margo Harrison/Shutterstock Images, 14-15; © Cameron Spencer/Getty Images for Red Bull, 16; © Chris Polk/AP Images, 17, 19; © Christian Petersen/Getty Images, 20; © Ricky Corey/iStockphoto, 21 (bottom); © Chris Roselli/ Shutterstock Images, 21 (center); © WilleeCole/Shutterstock Images, 21 (top); © Grant Hindsley/ AP Images, 22; © 26kot/Shutterstock Images, 23; © Jae C. Hong/AP Images, 24, 28; © Delly Carr/AP Images, 25; © Sportlibrary/Shutterstock Images, 26; © Warren Price Photography/ Shutterstock Images, 27; © John Miller/iStockphoto, 29.

Front cover: © Vaughn Youtz/ZUMA/CORBIS (main); © RTimages/Shutterstock.com (background).

Main body text set in Folio Std Light 11/17.
Typeface provided by Adobe Systems.

TABLE OF CONTENTS

CHAPTER ONE

WHAT IS MOTO X BEST TRICK?

In 1993 Bob Kohl became the first person to perform a backflip on a motocross bike. He knew the trick was awesome. But he didn't know that it would change the motocross world forever.

Before Kohl, motocross riders weren't sure if a backflip on a motorcycle was even possible. People were impressed when Kohl landed the trick on his Honda CR80 motocross bike. To flip and land on a motorcycle was an amazing stunt. But Kohl mastered that trick. And he paved the way for other new stunts. More people learned to flip. Daring riders tried to land flips on even bigger bikes than Kohl's. Riders kept pushing the limits of the backflip. They started combining flips with other tricks. Without Kohl and his bike, the explosion in motocross riding and best trick may never have happened.

Motocross riders still do backflips to show off for judges and fans.

Motocross bikes were originally motorcycles designed for racing on a dirt course. But eventually riders began using those dirt tracks for more than racing. They began performing tricks on the courses. In the ESPN X Games motocross best trick competition, professionals do stunts off big jumps. The best trick jumps are much larger than the jumps in a traditional motocross course. The tricks are more intense. The best trick competition is about daring to try new stunts.

Improvements in bikes allow riders to do bigger and better tricks than ever before.

Motocross has changed since the days of Kohl's first flip. The stunts have gotten bigger. The courses have changed. The bikes are lighter and sturdier. Thanks to sponsors such as Red Bull, best trick riders have become well known. These riders are heroes to their fans. All this means a future full of big tricks!

SAFETY FIRST!

Pushing limits means taking more risks. Motocross best trick is a dangerous sport. If a basketball player makes a mistake, that player might pull a muscle. If a rider makes a mistake in motocross best trick, the rider could die. This is a serious danger. Even the best riders make mistakes. Kohl performed backflips for two years. But in 1995, he crashed and was seriously injured. He recovered and was able to ride again. But the injury was a big setback in his career. Because of the risks, even professional motocross riders wear safety gear at all times.

CHAPTER TWO

THE BIRTH OF MOTOCROSS

Motocross riding was popular long before riders revved up their engines and flew off huge jumps. Motocross began in England in 1924 with an off-road event called Scrambles. In those days, motorcycles were simply bicycles with small engines. Riders raced on a 50-mile (80-kilometer) course. Motocross courses were made in fields and dirt lots. Every course was different. The event soon caught on in France. French riders added small jumps to their courses. They also gave the sport its name: motocross. For the next few decades, Europe was the home of motocross.

EVEL KNIEVEL

During the 1960s and the 1970s American stuntman Evel Knievel was the world's most famous daredevil. Knievel helped make freestyle motocross popular. He was known for death-defying motorcycle jumps. In 1975 he jumped over 14 Greyhound buses. It was a distance of 163 feet (50 meters). His big air got kids dreaming about the tricks they could do on their own dirt bikes.

Legendary stuntman Evel Knievel inspired motocross riders to try big tricks.

By the mid-1960s, motocross had made its way across the Atlantic Ocean. Early American motocross didn't feature the kinds of stunts Kohl would do in the 1990s. Americans held events known as supercross. The first U.S. supercross competition was held in Los Angeles, California, in 1972.

Supercross rider Bob Hannah won the 1977 AMA International Supercross championship.

Supercross brought motocross into indoor stadiums. These indoor courses gave the sport consistency. The tracks were man-made unlike the European courses. These tracks could be copied. Riders raced around tracks that had jumps and obstacles. The races were about speed and skill. Audiences could watch the sport from a comfortable stadium. From the beginning of supercross, riders wanted to catch more air (jump higher). They challenged themselves. They practiced new tricks on sand dunes and mountains.

The Rise of Freestyle and Modern Motocross

In 1999 the X Games hosted
its first freestyle motocross
competition. Unlike in supercross,
these riders weren't timed. Instead,
they performed multiple tricks on a
course with jumps. Fifteen-year-old
Travis Pastrana won the gold medal. That

same year, another extreme sports event known as the Gravity Games
also featured freestyle motocross for the first time. Again, Travis took
gold. Experienced freestyler Ronnie Faisst took silver. At the 2000 Gravity
Games, rider Carey Hart did the first backflip on a full-sized motocross
bike. The crowd went wild. But Hart crashed trying to make the landing.
Doing tricks on a bigger bike meant the rider had to handle a lot more
power and weight. This took skill but also let riders jump farther and
higher and stay in the air longer.

THE X GAMES

Since 1995 ESPN and now its sister station ABC have held
an action sports competition called the Extreme Games
(shortened to X Games). It is the most important competition
for extreme action sports such as motocross best trick. Like
the Olympic Games, X Games riders compete for medals.
Winners earn gold, silver, or bronze medals as well as prize
money. Pro riders typically work for months, if not all year,
trying to perfect a specific move. This is why the X Games
are a birthplace for many never-before-seen tricks.

Dan Pastor does a stunt at the 2002 X Games big air competition in Philadelphia, Pennsylvania. In 2004 the competition's name was changed to best trick.

In 2001 the X Games added a big air event. Soon the name was changed to best trick. In best trick, each rider gets two jumps to show off a trick that will wow the judges. Every year many brand-new tricks are performed at the X Games best trick competition.

TRAVIS PASTRANA

Travis Pastrana is a superstar of freestyle motocross. He was the first rider to land a double backflip. In 1999 Pastrana was the first person to win the motocross freestyle event at the X Games. His score of 99 out of 100 remains the highest ever in that event. He has won 10 medals at the X Games. Pastrana also started an action sports show called *Nitro Circus*. The show began as a miniseries, but MTV picked it up as a television series. The first episode aired in 2009. Pastrana is also a star in other action sports, including supercross, rally racing, monster truck freestyle, and NASCAR (National Association for Stock Car Auto Racing).

New and better bikes have allowed riders to use bigger jumps. Riders can also do tricks more safely. They practice new tricks by jumping into a pit of foam. This soft landing reduces the risk of injuries. Today's riders try for bigger and more exciting stunts than ever before. In 2011 rider Jackson "Jacko" Strong performed the first-ever front flip done at the X Games. With heroes such as Strong, Pastrana, and Faisst and stunts that keep getting better, motocross best trick seems here to stay.

Extreme sports star Travis Pastrana is one of the most famous athletes in moto X best trick.

13

CHAPTER THREE

MOTOCROSS BRANDS, EQUIPMENT, AND MOVES

Pro best trick riders need the right equipment. Brands play a huge role in freestyle motocross. Motocross best trick brands revolve around bikes, beverages, and clothing. For an amateur rider hoping to go pro, getting sponsored by one of these brands is an important career move. Without the brands, there would be no best trick competitions.

Motocross bikes are designed to be lightweight and very sturdy to handle rough landings.

Sponsoring brands such as Monster Energy Drink allow riders to compete professionally.

The Bikes

Best trick competitions couldn't exist without motorcycles. Many pros are very loyal to a certain brand of bike. Travis Pastrana only rides Suzuki bikes. In return, Suzuki sponsors him. The company helps support Pastrana financially. When Pastrana does an awesome trick on his bike, Suzuki gets some great advertising. Bike brands don't just help out the sport by sponsoring riders. These companies also invest millions of dollars in improving bikes. These new bikes are often lighter and safer. The better the bike, the better the trick.

Red Bull is a major sponsor of many different motocross freestyle events.

The Beverages

Beverage companies play an important role in best trick competitions. Companies such as Red Bull, Rockstar, Monster, and Mountain Dew sponsor motocross teams and events. Along with other sponsors, these companies allow riders to make motocross their full-time jobs. Once a rider becomes pro, he or she may get invited to events. The rider will be paid to show up and ride. If a rider wins the event, he or she gets paid even more money. Motocross is a risky sport. It takes a lot of practice to perform a trick safely. Riders love getting big air. But they wouldn't have time to practice if they needed another job to earn money. These beverage companies help support professional riders financially. This support allows the riders to focus on learning new tricks.

BRIAN DEEGAN

Brian Deegan turned pro in 1997 at the age of 17. During his rookie year, he won a race, then got off his bike to walk and dance behind it as the bike crossed the finish line. This move is known as ghost riding. Later in his career, Deegan founded Metal Mulisha. This clothing and accessories company is still very popular among motocross riders. On the bike, Deegan is known for being the first person to ever complete a 360 (a full-rotation spin) in a competition. He called the move the Mulisha twist. He has competed in multiple motocross events in every X Games from 1995 to 2012.

Brian Deegan's Metal Mulisha brand has become a major sponsor for many motocross riders.

The Style

Many pro riders create their own clothing brands and teams to sponsor riders. Riders Brian Deegan and Larry Linkogle started the Metal Mulisha clothing line. Ronnie Faisst started the Shui clothing line. Both brands feature the casual style motocross fans love. Many fans wear these brands at events. Both brands also sponsor riders. These side projects let pro riders earn money even when they are not healthy enough to ride.

Foam pits help riders practice new tricks safely. They are less likely to get injured or damage their bikes.

Equipment

Motocross gear can be expensive. Skateboarders only need to buy a skateboard and some safety gear. But in motocross best trick, riders need to buy a motorcycle. Motorcycles can be expensive. But the good news is that once a bike is set up, it is ready for almost any kind of motocross. A rider can do beginning or more advanced tricks on the same bike. Motocross bikes are different from normal motorcycles. Motocross bikes are much lighter than street bikes. They are built to withstand the huge shocks that come from landing big jumps.

The rider's experience and size are key considerations in choosing the right bike. The most important thing is finding a motorcycle with which the rider is comfortable. Being comfortable on a bike is the first step toward being safe.

Even pros take hard falls. Pro rider Scott Murray crashed during the best trick event at the 2007 X Games.

Safety

Being safe on a motocross bike starts with the rider knowing his or her bike well and feeling comfortable on it. But it doesn't end there. Best trick riders go for the biggest tricks possible. But landing these tricks is not easy. Crashes are bound to happen. Even pro riders often take a bad fall or slide out as they land. Because of these risks, pro riders recommend some must-have safety gear.

RONNIE FAISST'S
MUST-HAVE
SAFETY GEAR

GOGGLES

If riders can't see, they can't land jumps. Goggles protect a rider's eyes from the dust and sand that gets kicked up on dirt ramps.

NECK BRACE

Many pros also ride with a neck brace. The neck is incredibly fragile. If a rider gets a neck injury in a fall, he or she could be paralyzed for life or even die.

KNEE AND ELBOW GUARDS

While not all pros wear these, they are a good Idea. Many riders also choose to wear knee braces. These keep the knees from twisting on hard landings.

BOOTS

Motocross boots help protect a rider's feet, ankles, and shins. They are made with plastic or even steel to provide extra protection during best-trick riding.

HELMET

A helmet protects a rider's head. No rider can land a jump perfectly every time. Crashing is part of learning new tricks. Riders protect their skulls with a hard helmet. Most motocross helmets have bright designs. The graphics reflect a rider's personality and help the rider stand out to his or her fans.

GLOVES

When a rider falls, his or her hands are often the first things to hit the ground. Gloves protect a rider's hands from getting cut up on the dirt and gravel of the best trick ramp. They also help a rider grip his or her bike.

Rider Taka Higashino practices a nothing trick.

The Moves

No-Hander

A no-hander is when a rider lets go of his or her handlebars in midair.

No-Footer and Nothing

A no-footer is like a no-hander, but the rider takes his or her feet off the bike in midair. A rider can combine a no-footer with a no-hander to create a move known as a nothing.

Can Can

In a can can, the rider takes one foot off the peg. Then the pro brings the foot over to the other side of the bike so both legs are on one side of the bike. Some pros can even land the bike in this position.

Look Over

To do a look over, the rider takes both feet off the pegs and one hand off the handlebars. The rider's body is almost completely off the bike as the rider looks over his or her shoulder.

In a can can, a pro kicks both legs over one side of the bike.

BEST TRICK SCHOOLS

Unlike other extreme sports, motocross riders need a special place to train. Best trick jumpers need a lot of open space, a jump, and the right terrain. Best trick jumpers need a foam pit to practice big tricks without injuring themselves. Motocross best trick involves a lot of risk. The best way for a new rider to safely learn the sport is with the help of an expert teacher. Motocross schools across the country teach both kids and adults how to safely ride motocross and do tricks.

Nac-Nac

When doing a nac-nac, a rider turns the bike sideways. This move is
known as a whip. Then the rider takes one foot off the peg and swings
it over to the other side of the bike while airborne. This trick looks a lot
like a reverse can can. Some riders will try looking back to get a higher
score. At the 2011 X Games, rider Cam Sinclair combined a nac-nac with
a double backflip.

Most riders know Hart as the godfather of flips. He began riding when he was only six years old and turned pro when he was 18. Hart was the first motocross rider to land a flip in competition. Hart's signature move was one he created: the Hart attack. Hart's riding days ended as many pros' do: with an injury.

Superman

In a superman, the rider releases both feet from the pegs and kicks his or her feet straight back. To add to the trick, the rider might do a superman seat grab. In this move, the rider releases one hand and grabs the seat. Carey Hart invented a move known as the Hart attack. In the Hart attack, the rider does a superman with both legs pointed straight up in the air. Riders often combine two tricks to create moves called combos.

Carey Hart does a Hart attack in 1999.

CHAPTER FOUR

BECOMING A CHAMP

O f all the mainstream action sports, best trick motocross may be one of the most dangerous. Even with lots of practice, riders can be seriously injured or even die. Most freestyle riders will never get sponsored or picked up by a team. These riders don't ride to earn money or fame. They ride because they love the sport. But with enough hard work, a rider might become good enough to enter amateur competitions. At amateur competitions, a sponsor or a team may notice a talented rider. When a team or a company offers to sponsor a rider, the rider can ride professionally. Pro riders tend to have specialty moves. They practice these moves for months or even years to perfect them. For instance, Travis Pastrana is famous for his double backflip.

While most best trick riders love doing stunts for a crowd, they perform because they love the sport.

Women's motocross racing is a popular sport around the world.

Team Riding

Most pro riders are on a team sponsored by a company such as Monster or Red Bull. However everyone on those teams is an independent rider. Motocross best trick is an individual sport. Team members compete against one another.

WOMEN IN MOTOCROSS

Women's freestyle motocross is still a relatively new sport. In 2012 the X Games still had not introduced a women's class in the best trick competition. "Scary" Mary Perkins is one of the best-known female motocross stunt riders. She holds the world record for the longest jump by a female rider. Her motocross career ended in 2009 when she was seriously injured in a crash. She is now an inspirational speaker. Women's motocross racing is already a huge event at the X Games. A women's best trick event may be in the future.

Jacko Strong celebrates after landing his front flip at the 2011 X Games.

The Events

Each year a number of major events bring together the top motocross best trick riders. Red Bull sponsors several competitions throughout the year. The X Games and Mountain Dew's Dew Tour also take place every year. The Dew Tour also has an amateur series. Rookie riders who win in the amateur series have a shot at making it to the pro tour. Jacko Strong is one of the best riders in motocross best trick. In 2011 he wowed judges with a front flip. It was the first front flip ever landed in a competition. The move won him the gold medal. He also took gold in the 2012 X Games best trick competition.

JACKO STRONG

Jacko Strong represents a new class of riders who are pushing the limits. When Strong was only 15 years old, he became the youngest person to do a backflip on a full-sized motorcycle. His fearless riding earned him an invitation to join Brian Deegan's Metal Mulisha team. He took the gold medal in the 2011 and 2012 X Games.

Judging

In a best trick competition, riders are judged on both the difficulty of their moves and their style. If a rider makes his or her tricks as long and smooth as possible, that rider will get a high score for style. At the X Games, both difficulty and style are scored up to 50 points. A perfect score is 100 points. Riders only get two jumps. Whichever jump earns the rider the highest score is the rider's final score.

Where to Watch

ESPN's X Games is one of the easiest best trick competitions to watch. It is shown on national cable television and on the ABC network. Fans who don't want to wait for the competitions can have a parent or adult help them find videos online. Best trick highlights from pros and amateurs alike are available through video sharing websites such as YouTube. (Beginning riders need to be careful, however. Trying to copy moves shown online can be a quick way to get injured!)

When done safely, motocross best trick can be a fun and thrilling sport—even for a rookie.

GLOSSARY

AMATEUR
someone who participates in an activity for fun without expectation of payment

COMBOS
groups of tricks done together

DAREDEVIL
someone who enjoys risky activities

FREESTYLE
a type of motocross event where riders do tricks rather than race

MAINSTREAM
something that is normal or commonly accepted

PROFESSIONAL
someone who participates in an activity as a job for payment

ROOKIE
someone who is new to a sport or activity

SPONSOR
a company that financially supports an individual so he or she can focus on an activity

SUPERCROSS
a type of American motocross racing that takes place on an indoor course

TERRAIN
the features of an area of land

Further Reading

Cain, Patrick G. *Moto X Freestyle*. Minneapolis: Lerner Publications, 2013.

Woods, Bob. *Motocross History from Local Scrambling to World Championship MX to Freestyle*. New York: Crabtree, 2008.

Zuehlke, Jeffrey. *Motorcycle Road Racing*. Minneapolis: Lerner Publications, 2009.

Websites

ESPN X Games
http://espn.go.com/action/xgames
The official X Games website features information about the X Games. Check out motocross best trick athlete bios, videos, and scores, and find out when and where the next X Games will be held.

Freestyle Motocross
http://www.freestyle-motocross.net/
Visit this website to learn more about freestyle motocross and the kinds of tricks you might see at a best trick competition.

Heidi Henry Talks Motocross
http://www.kidzworld.com/article/3379-heidi-henry-talks-motocross#
Learn more about the exciting sport of freestyle motocross from famous rider Heidi Henry.

INDEX

About the Author

Patrick Cain is a nuclear engineer turned writer. He is an award-winning journalist whose work often appears in a number of magazines such as *ESPN the Magazine*, and *Fast Company*. He currently lives in Los Angeles, California, but will forever be tied to upstate New York.